Wild Animals

TIGER

Lionel Bender

Chrysalis Children's Books

First published in the UK in 2004 by
Chrysalis Children's Books
An imprint of Chrysalis Books Group Plc,
The Chrysalis Building, Bramley Road,
London W10 6SP

ISBN 1 84458 170 5

British Library Cataloguing in Publication Data
for this book is available from the British Library.

Editorial Manager *Joyce Bentley*
Senior Editor *Rasha Elsaeed*
Editorial Assistant *Camilla Lloyd*

Produced by Bender Richardson White
Project Editor *Lionel Bender*
Designer *Ben White*
Production *Kim Richardson*
Picture Researcher *Cathy Stastny*
Cover Make-up *Mike Pilley, Radius*

Printed in China

10 9 8 7 6 5 4 3 2 1

Words in **Bold** can be found in New words on page 31.

Typography *Natascha Frensch*
Read Regular, READ SMALLCAPS and Read Space; European Community Design Registration 2003 and Copyright © Natascha Frensch 2001-2004 Read Medium, **Read Black** and *Read Slanted*
Copyright © Natascha Frensch 2003-2004

READ™ is a revolutionary new typeface that will enchance children's understanding through clear, easily recognisable character shapes. With its evenly spaced and carefully designed characters, READ™ will help children at all stages to improve their literacy skills, and is ideal for young readers, reluctant readers and especially children with dyslexia.

Picture credits

Cover : © Digital Vision. © Digital Vision: pages 1, 2, 4, 7, 9, 14, 15, 16. © Corbis Images Inc.: pages 17 (Terry Whittaker, Frank Lane Picture Agency), 21 (Gallo Images), 25 (Robert Pickett), 27 (Corbis Images). © Frank Lane Picture Agency Limited: pages 6 (Jurgen & Christine Sohns), 8 (Mark Newman), 11 (Silvestris Fotoservice), 12 (Terry Whittaker), 13 (Gerard Lacz), 19 (David Hosking), 20 (Terry Whittaker), 22 (Gerard Lacz), 23 (Terry Whittaker), 24 (Robin Chillenden), 26 (Terry Whittaker), 29 (Mark Newman). © RSPCA Photolibrary: pages 5 (Mike Powles), 10 (Mike Powles), 18 (Cheryl A Erteit), 28 (Mike Powles).

Contents

Big cats

A tiger is a big cat. It is fiercer and wilder than a pet cat.

Tigers live in a few places in China, India, Russia and **South-east Asia.**

Homes

Most tigers live in forests. They stay close to water and where they can easily find food.

Some tigers live on **grasslands** or in **swamps**. Others live in snowy areas.

Food

The tiger is a meat eater.
It kills deer, wild pigs, monkeys
and snakes to eat.

A tiger that lives in swamps feeds on crabs and small crocodiles.

Hunting

A tiger hunts on its own, mostly when it is dark. It creeps up on its **prey** then pounces on it.

The tiger pushes its prey to the ground and breaks its neck.

Family life

A baby tiger is called a cub. It stays with its mother until it is two years old.

An adult tiger spends most of its time alone. When two adult males meet, they often fight.

Senses

The tiger has very good hearing, eyesight and smell. It uses these to hunt prey.

It uses its **whiskers** to feel its way in the dark.

Weapons

The tiger uses its four long, pointed teeth to kill animals and to tear off meat.

It uses its sharp **claws** to grip and tear **flesh**.

Tiger skin

A tiger's skin is covered in **fur**. The fur is brown or golden with black stripes.

The fur is the same colour and pattern as dry grass. This helps the tiger hide from its prey.

Baby tigers

A female tiger is called a tigress. She may give birth to between two and seven cubs.

Newborn cubs feed on their mother's milk. Later, the mother brings them meat to eat.

Growing up

Cubs love to run, jump and play.
They soon learn to hunt.

Sometimes the father tiger visits the cubs. He eats, sleeps and plays with the cubs.

Becoming an adult

The tiger is fully grown and ready to **breed** when it is three or four years old.

An adult tiger spends most of its time hunting or sleeping.

In danger

Tigers are threatened. Some people are cutting down forests, destroying tiger homes.

Other people kill tigers for their fur. They use the fur to make coats or rugs.

Tiger care

Scientists are studying tigers in the wild to find out how to help the animals survive.

Tiger homes are made into wildlife areas protected from farmers and fur traders.

Quiz

1 Where do tigers live?

2 Are tigers meat-eaters or plant-eaters?

3 Do tigers hunt during the day or when it is dark?

4 How many cubs does a mother
tiger have at a time?

5 At what age do young tigers leave their mother?

6 What are a tiger's main weapons?

7 What is an adult female tiger called?

8 Why do some people kill tigers?

The answers are all in this book!

New words

breed male and female getting together to make babies.

claws long, curved fingernails and toenails.

flesh skin and muscles of an animal.

fur thick hair that covers most of the body.

grasslands huge, open areas of grass dotted with trees.

prey an animal that is hunted and killed for food.

sense the way animals find out about their surroundings. Animals have five senses – sight, hearing, smell, taste and touch. The body senses something when it notices it is there.

South-east Asia part of the world between India and China and Australia. It includes such countries as Thailand and Malaysia and islands including Sumatra and Java.

swamps areas of grass and trees, in which the ground is full of water.

whiskers long hairs on each side of the face.

Index